PRAYERS FOR WORSHIP

Alternate Collects

PRAYERS FOR WORSHIP

Alternate Collects

Gregory J. Wismar
editor

Scripture taken from the HOLY BIBLE, NEW INTERNATIONAL VERSION®. Copyright © 1973, 1978, 1984 by International Bible Society. Used by permission of Zondervan Publishing House. All rights reserved.

The "NIV" and "New International Version" trademarks are registered in the United States Patent and Trademark Office by International Bible Society. Use of either trademark requires the permission of International Bible Society.

Copyright © 1993 Concordia Publishing House
3558 S. Jefferson Avenue, St. Louis, MO 63118-3968
Manufactured in the United States of America

All rights reserved. No part of this publication may be reproduced, stored in a retrieval system, or transmitted, in any form or by any means, electronic, mechanical, photocopying, recording, or otherwise, without the prior written permission of Concordia Publishing House.

Library of Congress Cataloging-in-Publication Data

Prayers for worship : alternate collects for the three year lectionary series / Gregory J. Wismar, editor.
    p. cm.
    ISBN 0-570-04610-6
    1. Lutheran Church—Missouri Synod—Prayer-books and devotions—English. 2. Lutheran Church—Prayer-books and devotions—English. 3. Church year—Prayer-books and devotions—English. I. Wismar, Gregory J., 1946–   .
BX8067.P7P73   1993
264'.041322013—dc20   93-12515

1   2   3   4   5   6   7   8   9   10   02   01   00   99   98   97   96   95   94   93

Contents

Foreword	7
The Advent Season	9
The Christmas Season	13
The Epiphany Season	14
The Sundays in Lent	23
Holy Week	28
The Easter Season	30
The Pentecost Season	37

Festivals and Days of Special Devotion:
    Christmas Eve, Christmas Day, Second Sunday after
    Christmas, Epiphany, Ash Wednesday, Good Friday
    Holy Saturday, Easter Eve, Ascension, Reformation
	69

Saints: Apostles, Evangelists, Men and Women of Faith	72
Life of the Church: Congregational Anniversary, Dedication, Celebration	73
Life of the Christian: Birth/Adoption of a Child, Marriage, Wedding Anniversary	74
Holidays: New Year, National Holiday, Thanksgiving	75

Foreword

"Let us pray . . . " These special words in the liturgy of the Church have drawn God's people at worship into a special moment of corporate prayer throughout the history of the Christian church. In liturgies from the first Christian centuries the Collect served as a conclusion to the Entrance Rite. It collected, or gathered together, the various petitions of the worshiping assembly into one brief, focused prayer, generally spoken by the presiding minister. As centuries passed, the prayer took on a specific form that included an addressing of one of the persons of the Holy Trinity, the petition, a reason for praying with trust, the desired result, and a doxological conclusion. The relating of the theme of the Collect to the liturgical day in the life of the Church was not always necessarily evident.

In recent usage the Collect has seen a change in function in many liturgies. Instead of collecting the people's prayer petitions expressed in the opening section of the service, it rather collects their prayer thoughts in anticipation of the proclamation of the Word. Now the most specific focus of the Collect in the worship of each Sunday and festival, in many settings, is to speak to God the thoughts and truths that will soon be heard in the reading of the appointed Gospel. The people of God collect their thoughts around the message to be read from the Scriptures, bringing that message to their lips before it reaches their ears.

The widespread use of the three-year lectionary has presented a challenge to those who would have a Collect fully appropriate to the readings of each week in the life of the Church, because current hymnals and altar books provide for each day only one Collect that must suffice for years A, B, and C. This volume, composed in response to a request from the Commission on Worship of The Lutheran Church—Missouri Synod, seeks to expand the corporate prayer options for the congregation by offering three Collects for each Sunday, one appropriate to Year A, one to Year B, and the last to Year C. Additional Collects for alternate use on days when only one set of readings has been appointed, as well as prayers for special occasions, are also included in this volume.

Selecting and crafting prayers for use by the people of God is a singular and responsible task. Grateful acknowledgement is extended to each of the contributors: the Rev. Paul L. Borgman (Year A), the Rev. Gerald P. Coleman (Year B), and Dr. Arthur A. Just, Jr. (Year C). Special thanks is also extended to Mary Cardella, who ably served as manuscript assistant. Finally, it should be noted that Collect form and wording from previous church worship resources have been utilized, where appropriate, in this collection.

May these Collects serve to enrich the shared faith and life of the people of God as they gather for worship. "Let us pray . . ."

GREGORY J. WISMAR, D. MIN.

First Sunday in Advent

Year A

Stir up our hearts, O Lord, to prepare the way of your only Son that, at his second coming, we may worship him in glory for all eternity. He lives and reigns with you and the Holy Spirit, one God, now and forever. **Amen.**

Year B

Almighty God, Judge and King, the whole creation waits for your coming. Come, Lord Jesus, with your grace and fill our lives with your presence. Use all of our time for your gracious purpose; for you live and reign with the Father and the Holy Spirit, one God, now and forever. **Amen.**

Year C

Stir up your power, O Lord, and come that by your protection we may be rescued from the threatening perils of our sins and be saved by your mighty deliverance; for you live and reign with the Father and the Holy Spirit, one God, now and forever. **Amen.**

Second Sunday in Advent

Year A

Stir up your power, O Lord, and come among us with great might. Because we are severely hindered by our sins, by your grace and mercy deliver us quickly through our Lord Jesus Christ, who lives and reigns with you and the Holy Spirit, one God, now and forever. **Amen.**

Year B

Almighty God, Judge and King, you sent John the Baptist to prepare the way for your coming. Come, Lord Jesus, with your grace and fill us with your Holy Spirit. Inhabit our lives and our dreams so that we may live as your people in the world; for you live and reign with the Father and the Holy Spirit, one God, now and forever. **Amen.**

Year C

Stir up our hearts, O Lord, to make ready the way of your only-begotten Son, that at his second coming we may worship him in purity; he lives and reigns with you and the Holy Spirit, now and forever. **Amen.**

Third Sunday in Advent

Year A

Almighty God, you called John the Baptist to give witness to the coming of your Son. Grant us wisdom to do your will today and so to witness to Christ's coming and to prepare his way; through the same Jesus Christ, your Son our Lord, who lives and reigns with you and the Holy Spirit, one God, now and forever. **Amen.**

Year B

Almighty God, Judge and King, you sent John the Baptist to proclaim the message of salvation in Christ. Come, Lord Jesus, with your grace and help us all our days to proclaim your salvation; for you live and reign with the Father and the Holy Spirit, one God, now and forever. **Amen.**

Year C

Almighty God, through John the Baptist, the forerunner of Christ, you once proclaimed salvation; now grant that we may know this salvation and serve you in holiness and righteousness all the days of our lives; through Jesus Christ, our Lord, who lives and reigns with you and the Holy Spirit, one God, now and forever. **Amen.**

Fourth Sunday in Advent

Year A

Stir up your power, O Lord, and come quickly. Protect us by your strength and save us from the threatening dangers of our sinful nature, for you live and reign with the Father and the Holy Spirit, one God, now and forever. **Amen.**

Year B

Almighty God, Judge and King, when the time had fully come, you sent your Son, born of a virgin, for us and for our salvation. Come, Lord Jesus, with your grace, to all the places of the world where people desperately need you. Come and give us the gift of yourself; for you live and reign with the Father and the Holy Spirit, one God, now and forever. **Amen.**

Year C

Stir up your power, O Lord, and come among us with great might; and because we are sorely hindered by our sins, let your bountiful grace and mercy speedily help and deliver us; through Jesus Christ, our Lord, who lives and reigns with you and the Holy Spirit, one God, now and forever. **Amen.**

First Sunday after Christmas

Year A

Merciful God, through the prophets you prepared the way for our salvation. Give us willing hearts to listen to their warnings and turn from our sins, that we may greet with joy the coming of our Redeemer, Jesus Christ, who lives and reigns with you, in the unity of the Holy Spirit, one God, now and forever. **Amen.**

Year B

Gracious Father, in your great love for the world you have given us the gift of your only Son as the light of the nations and the glory of Israel. Open our hearts to receive him and sanctify our lives to proclaim your grace through Jesus Christ, your Son, our Lord, who lives and reigns with you and the Holy Spirit one God, now and forever. **Amen.**

Year C

Lord Jesus, you stayed behind in your Father's house to listen to the teachers of the law and learn from them. Direct us in all our actions by your gracious favor and help us in all our works—begun, continued, and ended in your name—to glorify you and finally by your mercy to receive eternal life; for you live and reign with the Father and the Holy Spirit, one God, now and forever. **Amen.**

FIRST SUNDAY AFTER THE EPIPHANY
The Baptism of Our Lord

Year A

Father in heaven, at his baptism you proclaimed Jesus your beloved Son and anointed him with the Holy Spirit. Make all who are baptized in your name faithful to our calling as your children, and help us boldly to confess our Savior and inherit eternal life. We pray in Jesus' name, who lives and reigns with you and the same Spirit, one God, now and forever. **Amen.**

Year B

Gracious Father, through the baptism of Jesus you have shown that you are God-with-us. Through our baptism into his death, you have connected us to his life. Help us to give witness to all that you have done for us, through Jesus Christ your Son, our Lord, who lives and reigns with you and the Holy Spirit, one God, now and forever. **Amen.**

Year C

Father in heaven, as at his baptism in the Jordan River you once proclaimed Jesus your beloved Son and anointed him with the Holy Spirit, empower with your same Spirit all who are baptized to keep the covenant into which we have been called, boldly confess our Savior, and with him receive life eternal; through Jesus Christ, who lives and reigns with you and the Holy Spirit one God, now and forever. **Amen.**

Second Sunday after the Epiphany

Year A

Merciful Father, you have given your only Son as the sacrifice for our sin. Give us grace to receive the fruits of his redeeming work with thanksgiving and daily follow in his way, who lives and reigns with you and the Holy Spirit, one God, now and forever. **Amen.**

Year B

Gracious God, you sent your Son, the Word made flesh, to call us to yourself. Help us to hear your call and to follow where you lead through Jesus Christ, your Son our Lord, who lives and reigns with you and the Holy Spirit, one God, now and forever. **Amen.**

Year C

Almighty and eternal God, at the wedding of Cana in Galilee your Son, Jesus Christ, showed his divine power in a miraculous sign. Grant your people faith always to see the glory of Jesus hidden in the means of your grace, the Gospel and the Sacraments; through Jesus Christ, our Lord, who lives and reigns with you and the Holy Spirit, one God, now and forever. **Amen.**

Third Sunday after the Epiphany

Year A

Lord God, through the works of your Son you showed your glory and established your kingdom among us. Let us share the life of Jesus Christ who came to share our humanity and redeem us from our sin. He lives and reigns with you and the Holy Spirit, one God, now and forever. **Amen.**

Year B

O Lord our God, your Word summons us to discipleship. Give us grace to relinquish control of our lives, so that we may serve you only, faithfully fulfilling our part in your plan for the world; through Jesus Christ, your Son, our Lord, who lives and reigns with you and the Holy Spirit, one God, now and forever. **Amen.**

Year C

Set us free, Lord Christ, from the bondage of sin, sickness, and Satan that today we may live the abundant life of forgiveness you first proclaimed to the world in your sermon at Nazareth; for you live and reign with the Father, in the unity of the Holy Spirit, one God, now and forever. **Amen.**

Fourth Sunday after the Epiphany

Year A

Father of glory, you reveal your greatness in showing mercy. Send us as peacemakers and witnesses to all people, and fill our hearts with joy in your gift of salvation; through your Son, Jesus Christ our Lord, who lives and reigns with you and the Holy Spirit, one God, now and forever. **Amen.**

Year B

Lord of all, in wisdom you order all things mightily and tenderly. Your Word brings order out of chaos, light out of darkness, and life out of death. Move us to submit to your rule, so that by your grace, we may become instruments of order, light, and life, through Jesus Christ, your Son, our Lord, who lives and reigns with you and the Holy Spirit, one God, now and forever. **Amen.**

Year C

Almighty God, because your Son experienced rejection at his hometown of Nazareth, you know the perils and disappointments we face as your children. Graciously grant your strength and protection to support us in all dangers and carry us through all temptations; through our Lord Jesus Christ, your Son, who lives and reigns with you and the Holy Spirit, one God, now and forever. **Amen.**

Fifth Sunday after the Epiphany

Year A

Almighty God, you called us out of darkness into light so that we will show forth your praise in all the world; shine in our hearts; through Jesus Christ, your Son our Lord, who lives and reigns with you and the Holy Spirit, one God, now and forever. **Amen.**

Year B

O God of compassion, you sent your Son Jesus to move among your people with healing for every hurt of life. Send him among us with that same power to heal our sinful lives, through the same Jesus Christ, your Son our Lord, who lives and reigns with you and the Holy Spirit, one God, now and forever. **Amen.**

Year C

O God, our loving Father, through the grace of your Holy Spirit you call us, as you called the first disciples, to follow you as fishers of men. Make us to love you with our whole strength and with our whole heart and do the things that are pleasing in your sight; through Jesus Christ, your Son, our Lord, who lives and reigns with you and the Holy Spirit, one God, now and forever. **Amen.**

Sixth Sunday after the Epiphany

Year A

O Lord, we pray for your Spirit to guide us and to give us the grace and strength to do your will; through your Son, Jesus Christ our Lord, who lives and reigns with you and the Holy Spirit, one God, now and forever. **Amen.**

Year B

Merciful Father, as your Son, Jesus, reached out to embrace people with the healing power of your love, we ask that through us, you will also embrace all those you love, offering them the health of body, mind, and spirit that you alone can give; through your Son, Jesus Christ, our Lord, who lives and reigns with you and the Holy Spirit, one God, now and forever. **Amen.**

Year C

O Lord, you bless the poor, the hungry, the weeping, and the persecuted. Mercifully hear the prayers of your people when they call upon you, and give us faith to believe that your kingdom belongs to the humble of heart; through Jesus Christ, your Son, who lives and reigns with you and the Holy Spirit, one God, now and forever. **Amen.**

Seventh Sunday after the Epiphany

Year A

God of compassion, keep before us the love you have revealed through your Son, as he prayed for his enemies. Help us to be like him in our words and our deeds. We ask this through the same Jesus Christ our Lord, who lives and reigns with you and the Holy Spirit, one God, now and forever. **Amen.**

Year B

O Lord, you gave your Son Jesus power to heal and authority to forgive. Give to your servants both the healing of our illnesses and the forgiveness of our sins, through the same Jesus Christ, our Lord, who lives and reigns with you and the Holy Spirit, one God, now and forever. **Amen.**

Year C

O Lord, you taught us to love our enemies and to be merciful as you are merciful. By your Holy Spirit grant us the gifts of love and peace without which we cannot live before you; for the sake of your Son, Jesus Christ, who lives and reigns with you and the Holy Spirit, one God, now and forever. **Amen.**

Eighth Sunday after the Epiphany

Year A

Lord, help us not to be anxious about earthly things but to set our hearts on things heavenly. While we live among things that are passing away, strengthen our hold on what will endure in Jesus Christ our Lord, who lives and reigns with you and the Holy Spirit, one God, now and forever. **Amen.**

Year B

Everlasting Father, through your Son Jesus you have revealed your undeserved love for the world. Help your people to celebrate that far-reaching love in such a way that many shall accept your gracious invitation to the wedding feast that has no end; through the same Jesus Christ your Son, our Lord, who lives and reigns with you and the Holy Spirit, one God, now and forever. **Amen.**

Year C

Most loving Father, you have built your Church on the solid foundation of Jesus Christ, your Son, our Lord. Mercifully prepare us to hear his Word. Set us free from the bonds of our sins and defend us from all evil; through the same Jesus Christ your Son, who lives and reigns with you and the Holy Spirit, one God, now and forever. **Amen.**

The Transfiguration of Our Lord

Year A

O God, in the transfiguration of your Son, you confirmed the mysteries of the faith. In the voice from the bright cloud you also certified our adoption as your children and heirs of your glory. Bring us to the full joy of heaven; through the same Jesus Christ our Lord, who lives and reigns with you and the Holy Spirit, one God, now and forever. **Amen.**

Year B

God of grace and glory, before your Son turned his face to Jerusalem and Mount Calvary, on another mountain you revealed his glory. Sustain your Church both by his glory and also by your grace, and help us to reflect the glory of your love to all; through Jesus Christ, your Son, our Lord, who lives and reigns with you and the Holy Spirit, one God, now and forever. **Amen.**

Year C

O God, in the glorious transfiguration of your only-begotten Son you confirmed the mysteries of the faith, and in the voice that came from the bright cloud, you wondrously foreshowed our adoption by grace, as co-heirs with our King of his glory; bring us to the fullness of our inheritance in heaven; through Jesus Christ our Lord, who lives and reigns with you and the Holy Spirit, one God, now and forever. **Amen.**

First Sunday in Lent

Year A

Almighty God, your Son was led into the wilderness by the Spirit to be tempted by Satan. Come quickly to help us who, because of our weaknesses, are assaulted by many temptations. Give each one of us strength and victory through Jesus Christ our Lord, who lives and reigns with you and the Holy Spirit, one God, now and forever. **Amen.**

Year B

O Lord, God of Abraham, by the death and resurrection of your only Son you have shown the world that the way of self-sacrifice is the way of life. Give us such a strong faith in your providence that we will not shrink from any sacrifice you ask of us, but rejoice to offer our lives to him who gave his life for us, Jesus Christ, your Son, our Lord, who lives and reigns with you and the Holy Spirit, one God, now and forever. **Amen.**

Year C

O almighty and eternal God, we implore you to direct, sanctify, and govern our hearts and lives in the ways of your laws and the works of your commandments that through your mighty protection, both now and always, we may be preserved in body and in soul; through our Lord Jesus Christ, your Son, who lives and reigns with you and the Holy Spirit, one God, now and forever. **Amen.**

Second Sunday in Lent

Year A

O God, we give you glory because your mercy does not change. Be gracious to all who have gone astray and turned to their own ways, and bring them again with repentant hearts and steadfast faith to embrace the unchangeable truth of your Word, Jesus Christ your Son, who lives and reigns with you and the Holy Spirit, one God, now and forever. **Amen.**

Year B

Gracious Father, for the joy set before him, your Son Jesus endured the suffering of the cross. In our suffering, O Lord, strengthen our faith that we may know your companionship in our darkest hours, through your Son, Jesus Christ our Lord, who lives and reigns with you and the Holy Spirit, one God, now and forever. **Amen.**

Year C

O God, whose glory it is always to have mercy, be gracious to all who have gone astray from your ways, and bring them again with penitent hearts and steadfast faith to embrace and hold fast the unchangeable truth of your Word; through Jesus Christ, your Son, our Lord, who lives and reigns with you and the Holy Spirit, one God, now and forever. **Amen.**

Third Sunday in Lent

Year A

Almighty God, you show the light of your truth to those in darkness. Give strength to all who are joined in your family to reject what erodes their faith and to follow your Son, Jesus Christ our Lord, who lives and reigns with you and the Holy Spirit, one God, now and forever. **Amen.**

Year B

O Lord, you gave the Law so that even in our sin we might know your will for our lives, and you gave us your only Son to cleanse our lives of sin. For his sake, forgive us and renew us, so that we may serve you faithfully; through the same Jesus Christ, your Son, our Lord, who lives and reigns with you and the Holy Spirit, one God, now and forever. **Amen.**

Year C

Almighty God, because you know that we of ourselves have no strength, keep us both outwardly and inwardly that we may be defended from all adversities that may happen to the body and from all evil thoughts that may assault and hurt the soul; through Jesus Christ your Son, our Lord, who lives and reigns with you and the Holy Spirit, one God, now and forever. **Amen.**

Fourth Sunday in Lent

Year A

Heavenly Father, your Son came not to be served but to serve. As we follow in his steps, give us wisdom, patience, and courage to minister in his name to all who suffer and are in need; for the love of him who laid down his life for us, your Son our Savior Jesus Christ, who lives and reigns with you and the Holy Spirit, one God, now and forever. **Amen.**

Year B

Eternal God, you so loved the world that you gave your only Son into death for our sin. Take our lives, Lord, and use them to lift up your Son so that all will be drawn to him and find eternal life, for he lives and reigns with you and the Holy Spirit, one God, now and forever. **Amen.**

Year C

Almighty God, our Heavenly Father, your mercies are new every morning, and though we have in no way deserved your goodness, you still abundantly provide for all our wants of body and soul. Give us, we pray, your Holy Spirit that we may heartily acknowledge your merciful goodness toward us, give thanks for all your benefits, and serve you in willing obedience; through Jesus Christ, your Son, our Lord, who lives and reigns with you and the Holy Spirit, one God, now and forever. **Amen.**

Fifth Sunday in Lent

Year A

O God, by the suffering and death of your Son you redeemed this fallen world. Grant eternal joy to your faithful people, whom you have delivered from the danger of everlasting death, through the same Jesus Christ our Lord, who lives and reigns with you and the Holy Spirit, one God, now and forever. **Amen.**

Year B

God of love, you lifted up your Son on the cross so that you could draw all people to him. Fill us with thanksgiving for this incredible love that we dare to believe is ours. Help us to be faithful servants of your new covenant, reaching out to all those whom you claim; through Jesus Christ, your Son, our Lord, who lives and reigns with you and the Holy Spirit, one God, now and forever. **Amen.**

Year C

Almighty and eternal God, because it was your will that your Son should bear the pains of the cross for us so that the adversary can have no power over our lives; help us daily to remember our Lord's Passion and to rejoice in the remission of our sins and our redemption from everlasting death; through Jesus Christ, your Son, our Lord, who lives and reigns with you and the Holy Spirit, one God, now and forever. **Amen.**

SUNDAY OF THE PASSION
Palm Sunday

Year A

Everlasting God and Father, you sent your Son to take our flesh upon himself and to suffer death on the cross. Grant that, being inspired by his great humility and following his patient example, we may share in his victorious resurrection, who lives and reigns with you and the Holy Spirit, one God, now and forever. **Amen.**

Year B

Blessed are you, O Lord our God, King of the universe. You have poured out upon us your never-ending love by giving your Son Jesus Christ into death for us. He emptied himself and became obedient even to the death of the cross. Give us grace to share in his suffering and death so that we may be united with him in his resurrection. He lives and reigns with you and the Holy Spirit, one God, now and forever. **Amen.**

Year C

Almighty and everlasting God and Father, you sent your Son to take our nature upon himself and to suffer death on the cross that all should follow the example of his great humility; mercifully grant that we may both follow the example of our Savior Jesus Christ in his patience and also have our portion in his resurrection; through Jesus Christ, our Lord, who lives and reigns with you and the Holy Spirit, one God, now and forever. **Amen.**

Maundy Thursday

Year A

Holy God, source of love, on the night of his betrayal Jesus gave his disciples a new commandment: to love one another as he had loved them. By your Holy Spirit write this commandment on our hearts and in our lives. We pray through Jesus Christ our Lord, who lives and reigns with you and the Holy Spirit, one God, now and forever.
Amen.

Year B

Blessed are you, O Lord our God, King of the universe. You have poured out upon us your never-ending love by giving your Son Jesus Christ into death for us. Nourish your Church through the sacrament of his body and blood. Strengthen us so that we may continue to proclaim him who gives life to the world, for he lives and reigns with you and the Holy Spirit, one God, now and forever.
Amen.

Year C

O Lord Jesus, since you have left us a remembrance of your Passion in a wonderful sacrament, grant, we pray, that we may so participate in this sacrament of your body and blood that the fruits of your redeeming work may continually be manifest in us; for you live and reign with the Father and the Holy Spirit, one God, now and forever.
Amen.

EASTER DAY

The Resurrection of Our Lord

Year A

Almighty God, through your only Son, Jesus Christ, you overcame death and opened to us the gate of everlasting life. Save us from the death of sin by your life-giving Spirit; through Jesus Christ our Lord, who lives and reigns with you in the unity of the Holy Spirit, one God, now and forever. **Amen.**

Year B

Blessed are you, O Lord our God, King of the universe. In love you have given your Son, Jesus Christ, into death for us and raised him to life again; so raise us from the death of sin by your life-giving Spirit; through Jesus Christ our Lord, who lives and reigns with you and the Holy Spirit, one God, now and forever. **Amen.**

Year C

O God, for our redemption your only-begotten Son died on the cross, and by his glorious resurrection delivered us from the power of our enemy. Lead us to drown all our sins through daily repentance, that day by day a new person may arise to live before you in righteousness and purity forever; through Jesus Christ, our Lord, who lives and reigns with you and the Holy Spirit, one God, now and forever. **Amen.**

Second Sunday of Easter

Year A

Almighty God, we have celebrated the mystery of our Lord's resurrection from the dead. Help us to show the power of his resurrection in all that we say and do; through your Son, Jesus Christ, who lives and reigns with you and the Holy Spirit, one God, now and forever. **Amen.**

Year B

Risen and ascended Lord, you are alive forevermore. Increase our faith and inspire our witness. Fill your Church with the power of your resurrection to labor faithfully in joy until every tongue confesses, "My Lord and my God"; for you live and reign with the Father and the Holy Spirit, one God, now and forever. **Amen.**

Year C

Almighty God, your crucified and risen Son appeared to the disciples to strengthen their faith and give them the Holy Spirit to forgive and retain sin. Help us, who have celebrated the mystery of the Lord's resurrection, continually to receive the forgiveness of our sins; through Jesus Christ, our Lord, who lives and reigns with you and the Holy Spirit, one God, now and forever. **Amen.**

Third Sunday of Easter

Year A

O God, your Son made himself known to his disciples in the breaking of bread. Through the gift of faith open our eyes to behold him in all his redeeming work, who lives and reigns with you and the Holy Spirit, one God, now and forever. **Amen.**

Year B

Risen and ascended Lord, you have commanded us to preach repentance and forgiveness of sins to all nations. To fulfill this command, we ask you to clothe us with power from on high, your Holy Spirit, that we may carry the message of your resurrection to the ends of the earth; for you live and reign with the Father and the Holy Spirit, one God, now and forever. **Amen.**

Year C

Living Lord, you invite to your feast your disciples of all time. Assure us that our redemption is complete and give us the will to show forth in our lives what we profess with our lips; for you live and reign with the Father and the Holy Spirit, one God, now and forever. **Amen**

Fourth Sunday of Easter

Year A

O God, your Son is the Shepherd of your people. Grant that, when we hear his call, we will know his voice and follow where he leads; who, with you and the Holy Spirit, lives and reigns, one God, now and forever. **Amen.**

Year B

Risen and ascended Lord, you are the good Shepherd. You lay down your life for the sheep; they are yours. Empower your Church to reach every sheep of yours and to give witness until you have brought all your sheep into one fold; for you live and reign with the Father and the Holy Spirit, one God, now and forever. **Amen.**

Year C

Almighty God, merciful Father, since you brought back from the dead the Shepherd of your sheep, grant us your Holy Spirit to know his voice and to follow him, that sin and death may never pluck us out of your hand; through the same Jesus Christ, our Lord, who lives and reigns with you and the Holy Spirit, one God, now and forever. **Amen.**

Fifth Sunday of Easter

Year A

Almighty God, your Son, Jesus Christ, is the Way, the Truth, and the Life. Help us to be faithful to him to death and to receive life eternal. He lives and reigns with you and the Holy Spirit, one God, now and forever. **Amen.**

Year B

Risen and ascended Lord, you are the vine and we are the branches. Apart from you there is no life. By Baptism you have grafted us into your gracious life. Cause your Word to abide in us and make us fruitful to the glory of your Father, who lives and reigns with you and the Holy Spirit, one God, now and forever. **Amen.**

Year C

O God, your Son gave us the new commandment to love one another as he has loved us. Pour into our hearts, by your Holy Spirit, love of your commands and a desire for all that you promise, that among the manifold changes of this age our hearts may be fixed where true joys are to be found; through Jesus Christ, your Son, our Lord, who lives and reigns with you and the Holy Spirit, one God, now and forever. **Amen.**

Sixth Sunday of Easter

Year A

Almighty and eternal God, you have assured us that our redemption is complete through the resurrection of your Son. Give us the will to do in our lives what we profess with our lips; through the same Jesus Christ our Lord, who lives and reigns with you and the Holy Spirit, one God, now and forever. **Amen.**

Year B

Risen and ascended Lord, while we were still in our sins you chose us, laid down your life for us, and called us friends. By your great love for us, inspire us to love one another and to go out into the world to bear fruit according to your promise; for you live and reign with the Father and the Holy Spirit, one God, now and forever. **Amen.**

Year C

O Almighty God, you sent your Holy Spirit to teach us all things and bring to our remembrance the words of your Son, our Lord Jesus Christ. Give peace to our troubled hearts that we may receive your promises and with all your saints offer you our adoration and praise; through Jesus Christ, our Lord, who lives and reigns with you and the Holy Spirit, one God, now and forever. **Amen.**

Seventh Sunday of Easter

Year A

Almighty Father, your Son prayed for his disciples to remain one, as you and he are one. Keep your Church bound together in love and obedience to you, so that the world may believe in him whom you have sent, Jesus Christ our Lord, who lives and reigns with you and the Holy Spirit, one God, now and forever. **Amen.**

Year B

Risen and ascended Lord, you now pray for us at the throne of the Father. Keep all those whom you love in your name, O Lord, that they may be one even as you and the Father are one; for you live and reign with the Father and the Holy Spirit, one God, now and forever. **Amen.**

Year C

O King of glory, Lord of hosts, uplifted in triumph far above all heavens: Leave us not without consolation, but send us the Spirit of truth, whom you promised from the Father, that we may all be one, even as you and the Father are one; for you live and reign with the Father, in the unity of the Holy Spirit, one God, now and forever. **Amen.**

The Day of Pentecost

Year A

O God, on this day you taught the hearts of your faithful people by sending them the light of your Holy Spirit. Grant that by the same Spirit we have right judgment in all things and always rejoice in his holy strengthening; through Jesus Christ, your Son, our Lord, who lives and reigns with you, in the unity of the Holy Spirit, one God, now and forever. **Amen.**

Year B

O Holy Spirit, Lord and giver of life, breathe your life into our dry bones and into all your Church. Quench our thirst with the living water that flows from our Lord Jesus Christ, and channel those streams through us to everyone who is thirsty. For he lives and reigns with the Father and the Holy Spirit, one God, now and forever. **Amen.**

Year C

O God, on this day you once taught your faithful people by sending them your Holy Spirit. By your same Spirit give us a right understanding in all things and joy in his holy consolation; through Jesus Christ, your Son, our Lord, who lives and reigns with you in communion with the same Holy Spirit, one God, now and forever. **Amen.**

FIRST SUNDAY AFTER PENTECOST
The Holy Trinity

Year A

Almighty God our Father, dwelling in majesty and filling creation with your Spirit, reveal your glory through our Lord Jesus Christ, cleanse us from doubt and fear and send us boldly into all the world to worship you, with your Son and the Holy Spirit, one God, living and reigning, now and forever. **Amen.**

Year B

Gracious God, Father, Son, and Holy Spirit, at the creation of the world you turned chaos into order. At the wedding in Cana you turned water into wine. At Calvary and at Jesus' empty grave you turned death into life. Give us grace, like clay vessels, to carry your Good News to all nations until people everywhere worship you as the Giver of every good gift; for you live and reign, one God, now and forever. **Amen.**

Year C

Almighty and everlasting God, since you have given us, your servants, grace to acknowledge the glory of the eternal Trinity by the confession of the true faith and to worship the true Unity in the power of your divine majesty, keep us also steadfast in this true faith and worship and defend us ever from all our adversaries; for you, O Father, Son, and Holy Spirit, live and reign, one God, now and forever. **Amen.**

Pentecost 2

Year A

O Lord, without you we cannot do anything that is good; we ask for your Spirit to guide our thinking and to help us do what is pleasing to you. Enable us to live according to your will in your Son, Jesus Christ our Lord, who lives and reigns with you and the Holy Spirit, one God, now and forever. **Amen.**

Year B

Eternal God, your Son Jesus Christ is our true Sabbath rest. Help us to regard your Law as a gracious gift that points to him, and help us to attend to your Word in a way that honors him and pleases you; for he lives and reigns with you and the Holy Spirit, one God, now and forever. **Amen.**

Year C

O God, you give faith to believe in the healing power of your Word: Put away from us, we entreat you, temptations to doubt your providential care and give us those things that are profitable for our salvation; through Jesus Christ, our Lord, who lives and reigns with you and the Holy Spirit, one God, now and forever. **Amen.**

Pentecost 3

Year A

Lord and Giver of all good things, plant in our hearts the love of Your name, increase in us true religion, nourish us with your goodness, and produce in us the fruit of good works, through Jesus Christ our Lord, who lives and reigns with you and the Holy Spirit, one God, now and forever. **Amen.**

Year B

Almighty and eternal God, your Son Jesus triumphed over Satan and freed us from our bondage to sin. Rule our lives, enable us to do your will, and help others to see that we belong to you; through Jesus Christ, your Son, our Lord, who lives and reigns with you and the Holy Spirit, one God, now and forever. **Amen.**

Year C

O Lord, great prophet in word and deed, visit us with your redemption, heal our diseases, cleanse us from our sins, and give us hope in the resurrection of the dead, that by your holy inspiration we may glorify you and serve you in confidence and peace; for you live and reign with the Father and the Holy Spirit, one God, now and forever. **Amen.**

Pentecost 4

Year A

God our Savior, multitudes do not know the redeeming work of our Savior Jesus Christ. By the prayers and labors of your Church, lead all people to know and worship you through your Son, who lives and reigns with you and the Holy Spirit, one God, now and forever. **Amen.**

Year B

Gracious Father, in Jesus Christ your Son, you have inaugurated your kingdom of forgiveness and spiritual power. We pray that your kingdom will also come through us to others; through Jesus Christ, your Son, our Lord, who lives and reigns with you and the Holy Spirit, one God, now and forever. **Amen.**

Year C

Almighty and everlasting God, you sent your Son to forgive the sins of society's outcasts who turn to you in faith. Give us an increase in faith to receive the forgiveness you have promised and to love what you have commanded; through Jesus Christ, your Son, our Lord, who lives and reigns with you and the Holy Spirit, one God, now and forever. **Amen.**

Pentecost 5

Year A

Lord Almighty, Protector of your people, help us to leave behind our lethargy and fear, so that we will be faithful in the confession of your name to people everywhere; through the same Jesus Christ, your Son, our Lord, who lives and reigns with you and the Holy Spirit, one God, now and forever. **Amen.**

Year B

Almighty God, the powers of the universe are subject to you. Help us to find peace in your Lordship, through your Son, Jesus Christ, our Lord, who lives and reigns with you and the Holy Spirit, one God, now and forever. **Amen.**

Year C

O Lord, the Christ of God, your suffering, death, and resurrection opened to us everlasting life. Guide and govern us by your Holy Spirit to worship you in steadfast love, to revere and adore your holy name, and to follow in the way of your cross; for you live and reign with the Father and the Holy Spirit, one God, now and forever. **Amen.**

Pentecost 6

Year A

Lord Jesus, you demand unswerving devotion in your kingdom. Help us to find peace and fulfillment in giving without counting the cost. You live and reign with the Father and the Holy Spirit, one God, now and forever. **Amen.**

Year B

Almighty God, the powers of life and death are subject to your Lordship. Where there is illness, give us health. Where there is death, bring forth life. In all things, give us peace in knowing that nothing can separate us from your love for us that is in Christ Jesus our Lord, who lives and reigns with you and the Holy Spirit, one God, now and forever. **Amen.**

Year C

Heavenly Father, as Jesus set out resolutely for Jerusalem, there to suffer and die for the world; give us the strength to accept your schedule and to follow your agenda, that loving you above all things, we may obtain your promises, which exceed all that we can desire; through Jesus Christ, our Lord, who lives and reigns with you and the Holy Spirit, one God, now and forever. **Amen.**

Pentecost 7

Year A

Lord God, through your Son's humility you have revealed your salvation to us. Because sin burdens us and the troubles of the day weigh upon us, give us the rest you promise through Jesus Christ our Lord, who lives and reigns with you and the Holy Spirit, one God, now and forever. **Amen.**

Year B

Gracious Lord, your Son Jesus faithfully proclaimed your will and Word wherever he went. Grant that we too may be faithful in our proclamations, even among those who dishonor your Word, until your love reaches all those for whom your Son gave his life. For he lives and reigns with you and the Holy Spirit, one God, now and forever. **Amen.**

Year C

Almighty God, your Church is built on the foundation of the prophets and the apostles, Jesus Christ being the chief cornerstone. Give us ears to hear you proclaim through today's messengers of peace that Satan has been defeated and that our names are written in heaven; through Jesus Christ, our Lord, who lives and reigns with you and the Holy Spirit, one God, now and forever. **Amen.**

Pentecost 8

Year A

Almighty God, we thank you for planting in us the seed of your Word. By your Holy Spirit help us receive it with joy, live according to it, and grow into the full maturity of Christ, who lives and reigns with you in the unity of the Holy Spirit, one God, now and forever. **Amen.**

Year B

O God, your Son Jesus called disciples and sent them out with the authority of the Word. Help us to dare to believe that you have called us and sent us out with that same authority to bring many to the love of your name; through the same Jesus Christ, your Son, our Lord, who lives and reigns with you and the Holy Spirit, one God, now and forever. **Amen.**

Year C

O almighty and most merciful God, You teach us to love you with our whole heart and our neighbor as ourself. Through your bountiful goodness continue to fill us with compassion for those who are suffering, that we, being ready in body and soul, may cheerfully accomplish whatever things you want done; through Jesus Christ, your Son, our Lord, who lives and reigns with you and the Holy Spirit, one God, now and forever. **Amen.**

Pentecost 9

Year A

Our King and Redeemer, give us strength to cast away the works of darkness and put on the armor of light, so that when your Son comes again in glory to judge both the living and the dead, we may shine like the stars in glory; through him who lives and reigns with you and the Holy Spirit, one God, now and forever. **Amen.**

Year B

God of compassion, when you saw that we were like sheep without a shepherd, you sent your Son, Jesus, to shepherd us. Keep alive in us your spirit of compassion for the world, until all people come to know your Shepherd's care; through the same Jesus Christ, your Son, our Lord, who lives and reigns with you and the Holy Spirit, one God, now and forever. **Amen.**

Year C

Grant us, Lord, the Spirit to hear your Word and to know the one thing needful, so that we who without you cannot do anything that is good, by you will be able to choose the good portion; through Jesus Christ, your Son, our Lord, who lives and reigns with you and the Holy Spirit, one God, now and forever. **Amen.**

Pentecost 10

Year A

O God, you make your power known by showing mercy. Grant us your grace always to enjoy your heavenly Treasure, Jesus Christ our Lord, who lives and reigns with you and the Holy Spirit, one God, now and forever. **Amen.**

Year B

Gracious God, you provide for our needs in miraculous ways. Help us to trust in your provision for us and for all to whom you send us, through Jesus Christ, your Son, our Lord, who lives and reigns with you and the Holy Spirit, one God, now and forever. **Amen.**

Year C

O God, the Giver of all good things, teach us to ask of you those things we need for our salvation, that we may so pass through things temporal that we lose not the things eternal; through Jesus Christ, your Son, our Lord, who lives and reigns with you and the Holy Spirit, one God, now and forever. **Amen.**

Pentecost 11

Year A

Our Heavenly Father, though we do not deserve your goodness, still you provide for all our needs of body and soul. Pour out upon us your Holy Spirit to help us acknowledge your goodness, give thanks for all your benefits, and serve you obediently; through Jesus Christ your Son, our Lord, who lives and reigns with you in the unity of the Holy Spirit, one God, now and forever. **Amen.**

Year B

Everlasting Father, you have given your Son Jesus as the Bread of life for the world. Increase our hunger for him and our commitment to take him to all who hunger, until everyone knows the sustaining power of your love; through the same Jesus Christ, your Son, our Lord, who lives and reigns with you and the Holy Spirit, one God, now and forever. **Amen.**

Year C

Lord Jesus, you have laid up for us treasures in heaven. In your continual mercy, cleanse and defend us that we remain rich toward God; and because we cannot continue in safety without your help, govern and protect us always by your goodness; for you live and reign with the Father and the Holy Spirit, one God, now and forever. **Amen.**

Pentecost 12

Year A

Almighty and ever-living God, in your Son you have given great and precious promises to all who believe. Grant us faith that overcomes all doubts, through the same Jesus Christ our Lord, who lives and reigns with you and the Holy Spirit, one God, now and forever. **Amen.**

Year B

Eternal God, your Son Jesus is the Bread that comes down from heaven that we may eat and not die. Give to all who feast on him boldness to serve you without fear, through the same Jesus Christ, your Son, our Lord, who lives and reigns with you and the Holy Spirit, one God, now and forever. **Amen.**

Year C

Almighty and everlasting God, always more ready to hear than we are to pray, and always ready to give more than we either desire or deserve, prepare us for the coming of the Son of Man, forgiving us the things of which our conscience is afraid and giving us the good things we are not worthy to ask except through the merits and mediation of Jesus Christ, your Son, our Lord, who lives and reigns with you and the Holy Spirit, one God, now and forever. **Amen.**

Pentecost 13

Year A

Our Lord Jesus, you have endured the foolish questions and demands of every generation. Forgive us for trying to judge you, and help us likewise to accept all people as our brothers and sisters. You live and reign with the Father and the Holy Spirit, one God, now and forever. **Amen.**

Year B

Merciful God, you give eternal life to all who eat the body and blood of your Son, Jesus. Give us faith that will never be ashamed of him, but will take courage from his presence in our lives; who lives and reigns with you and the Holy Spirit, one God, now and forever. **Amen.**

Year C

Merciful Father, since you sent your only Son to undergo a singular baptism as the sacrifice for our sin, give us grace to receive with thanksgiving the fruits of his redeeming work and to follow in his way; through Jesus Christ, our Lord, who lives and reigns with you and the Holy Spirit, one God, now and forever. **Amen.**

Pentecost 14

Year A

Almighty God, you inspired Peter to confess Jesus as the Christ, your living Son. Keep your Church firm on the rock of this faith, that in unity and peace he will be proclaimed as Savior, who lives and reigns with you and the Holy Spirit, one God, now and forever. **Amen.**

Year B

Gracious God, Father of our Lord Jesus Christ, in him you have given us the words of eternal life. Increase our desire for his companionship and make us bold to confess him as the Holy One of God; for he lives and reigns with you and the Holy Spirit, one God, now and forever. **Amen.**

Year C

Lord of the banquet, grant us without all doubt to know you as the narrow door that leads to the eternal feast, where we shall see Abraham, Isaac, and Jacob and all the prophets in the kingdom of God; for you live and reign with the Father and the Holy Spirit, one God, now and forever. **Amen.**

Pentecost 15

Year A

Almighty God, your Son willingly endured the agony and shame of the cross for our redemption. Grant us courage to take up our cross and follow him wherever he leads, who lives and reigns with you and the Holy Spirit, one God, now and forever. **Amen.**

Year B

Almighty and eternal God, to know your Son, Jesus, is life. Give us the grace to know him and to worship you in spirit and in truth. Conform our lives to your design, and cast away from us everything that hinders our true worship; through Jesus Christ, your Son, our Lord, who lives and reigns with you and the Holy Spirit, one God, now and forever. **Amen.**

Year C

Holy One, higher than the proudest person, yet always bending down to the lowly, graft in our hearts the love of your name, increase in us true religion, nourish us with all goodness, and bring forth in us the fruit of good works; through Jesus Christ, your Son, our Lord, who lives and reigns with you and the Holy Spirit, one God, now and forever. **Amen.**

Pentecost 16

Year A

Almighty God, our Redeemer, in our weakness we have failed to be your messengers of forgiveness in the world and in your Church. Renew our concern for each other and our commitment to proclaim your reign of love; through your Son, Jesus Christ our Lord, who lives and reigns with you and the Holy Spirit, one God, now and forever. **Amen.**

Year B

God of compassion, your Son, Jesus, came to the suffering, the infirm, and the dying, and by his word of authority he set them free. Bless the ministry of your Church that it may continue to speak a word of deliverance to all those in need; through your Son, Jesus Christ, our Lord, who lives and reigns with you and the Holy Spirit, one God, now and forever. **Amen.**

Year C

Grant, merciful Lord, pardon and peace to your faithful people as they bear your cross and follow you as your disciples. Cleanse us from our sins to serve you with a quiet mind, who lives and reigns with the Father and the Holy Spirit, one God, now and forever. **Amen.**

Pentecost 17

Year A

O God, you reveal your power by showing mercy and love. Grant us your grace to receive what you have promised and to forgive as we have been forgiven through your Son, Jesus Christ our Lord, who lives and reigns with you and the Holy Spirit, one God, now and forever. **Amen.**

Year B

Eternal God, your Son, Jesus, is the Christ, the one anointed for the nations and our Savior. He is the Lamb of God who embraced the way of the cross to redeem us. Grant us faith to embrace the way of the cross as our way of life and to declare his redemptive presence to our world; for he lives and reigns with you and the Holy Spirit, one God, now and forever. **Amen.**

Year C

O God, your Son received sinners and ate with them, rejoicing in their repentance. We ask for your Holy Spirit to direct and govern our hearts, to lead us to repent of our sins and to receive forgiveness in the blessed sacrament of Christ's body and blood; through the same Jesus Christ, our Lord, who lives and reigns with you and the Holy Spirit, one God, now and forever. **Amen.**

Pentecost 18

Year A

Lord God, you call us to work in your vineyard. Supply us with diligence for tasks in your kingdom, always rejoicing with those to whom your Spirit has come; through Jesus Christ our Lord, who lives and reigns with you and the Holy Spirit, one God, now and forever. **Amen.**

Year B

God of love, in his ministry your Son, Jesus, put the needs of others ahead of his own. Keep us from thinking of ourselves more highly than we ought, and help us to mirror Christ's love that seeks the good of others; through the same Jesus Christ, your Son, our Lord, who lives and reigns with you and the Holy Spirit, one God, now and forever. **Amen.**

Year C

O Lord, you call us to be faithful in very little in order to be trusted with much. Preserve us by your perpetual mercy, and because without you we cannot but fall, keep us from all things hurtful and lead us to all things profitable to our salvation; for you live and reign with the Father and the Holy Spirit, one God, now and forever. **Amen.**

Pentecost 19

Year A

O God, the strength of all who put their trust in you, because of the weakness of our sinful nature we can do nothing to earn salvation. Grant us the help of your grace that we may please you with faith and obedience; through Jesus Christ, your Son, our Lord, who lives and reigns with you and the Holy Spirit, one God, now and forever. **Amen.**

Year B

Father of our Lord Jesus, the strength of all who trust you, help us to live according to your design and to treasure both your word of command and your word of forgiveness. Make our lives to be signs of your life and the instruments of renewal in our world; through your Son, Jesus Christ, our Lord, who lives and reigns with you and the Holy Spirit, one God, now and forever. **Amen.**

Year C

O God, through Moses and the prophets you proclaimed the way of everlasting life: grant us the fullness of your grace that with Lazarus we may obtain your promises and partake of your heavenly treasures; through Jesus Christ, your Son, our Lord, who lives and reigns with you and the Holy Spirit, one God, now and forever. **Amen.**

Pentecost 20

Year A

Almighty God, we, your servants, trusting not in our own merits, pray that you will not deal with us as we deserve but according to your mercy in Jesus Christ our Lord, who lives and reigns with you and the Holy Spirit, one God, now and forever. **Amen.**

Year B

Soften our hardness of heart, Lord God, that we may love all whom you love. Continue transforming our lives into invitations that summon people to the love of Christ, so that your full blessing may come to all for whom he died. He lives and reigns with you and the Holy Spirit, one God, now and forever. **Amen.**

Year C

O God, your almighty power is made known chiefly in showing mercy and pity. Teach us to forgive one another and to do what you have commanded, and because through the weakness of our mortal nature we can do no good thing without your aid, grant us the help of your grace to please you in both will and deed; through Jesus Christ, our Lord, who lives and reigns with you and the Holy Spirit, one God, now and forever. **Amen.**

Pentecost 21

Year A

Remember us, O Lord, not for what we deserve, but because you have begun your good work in us. As you have called us to your service, make us worthy of our calling; through your Son, Jesus Christ our Lord, who lives and reigns with you and the Holy Spirit, one God, now and forever. **Amen.**

Year B

Gracious Lord of all, let nothing interfere with our commitment to you. Give us that sense of priority that values all things properly and treasures nothing above Jesus Christ, who lives and reigns with you and the Holy Spirit, one God, now and forever. **Amen.**

Year C

Almighty Father, your Son came into the world to destroy the works of Satan and to make us your children and heirs of everlasting life. We give thanks to you for our redemption and for your promise to lead us into all truth; through Jesus Christ, your Son, our Lord, who lives and reigns with you and the Holy Spirit, one God, now and forever. **Amen.**

Pentecost 22

Year A

Lord of all, govern the nations of the world so that your Church may joyfully serve you in confidence and peace; through Jesus Christ our Lord, who lives and reigns with you and the Holy Spirit, one God, now and forever. **Amen.**

Year B

Lord God, your Son came not to be served but to serve, and to give his life as a ransom for many. Grant us grace to follow his example and to be his companions in service, that we may also share in his eternal reward; for he lives and reigns with you and the Holy Spirit, one God, now and forever. **Amen.**

Year C

Lord, give us grace to be persistent in our prayers for vindication from our enemies and to be given continuously to good works; through Jesus Christ, your Son, our Lord, who lives and reigns with you and the Holy Spirit, one God, now and forever. **Amen.**

Pentecost 23

Year A

O God, you teach us that loving you and our neighbor fulfills all your commandments. Give us wholehearted devotion to you, and unite us to one another with true charity; through your Son, Jesus Christ our Lord, who lives and reigns with you and the Holy Spirit, one God, now and forever.

Year B

Lord Jesus Christ, as you journeyed to your own suffering and death in Jerusalem, you stopped to heal blind Bartimaeus because you care for the hurts of both body and soul and desire our well-being at great cost to yourself. Help us to mirror your love to the world, for you live and reign with the Father and the Holy Spirit, one God, now and forever. **Amen.**

Year C

Almighty God, we pray, show us, your humble servants, your mercy for we put no trust in our own merits. Deal with us not according to the severity of your judgment but according to your mercy; through Jesus Christ, your Son, our Lord, who lives and reigns with you and the holy Spirit, one God, now and forever. **Amen.**

Pentecost 24

Year A

Lord, when the Day of Judgment comes, our only hope will be your grace. Keep us alert and watchful for Jesus' return, and for his sake invite us to his marriage feast, who lives and reigns with you and the Holy Spirit, one God, now and forever. **Amen.**

Year B

God of the covenant, you desire mercy and not sacrifice. Help us to love you with all that we have and all that we are, and to love our neighbors as ourselves; through Jesus Christ, your Son, our Lord, who lives and reigns with you and the Holy Spirit, one God, now and forever. **Amen.**

Year C

Lord Jesus Christ, you came to seek and to save the lost. Be present in our worship to grant us your salvation and to cleanse our thoughts and minds, making us a fit dwelling place; for you live and reign with the Father and the Holy Spirit, one God, now and forever. **Amen.**

Pentecost 25

Year A

Stir us, O Lord, more eagerly to seek the help you offer so that, when your Son, Jesus Christ, comes again in glory, we will enjoy all the blessings of salvation in him, who lives and reigns with you and the Holy Spirit, one God, now and forever. **Amen.**

Year B

Everlasting God, you did not hesitate to give your all for us. Awaken in us the desire to give our all for you and for your kingdom, through Jesus Christ, your greatest gift, who lives and reigns with you and the Holy Spirit, one God, now and forever. **Amen.**

Year C

O Lord, the God of Abraham and Isaac and Jacob, you are not the God of the dead, but of the living. Rule and govern our hearts and minds by your Holy Spirit, keeping us ever mindful of the resurrection of the dead and of your just judgment, ready to dwell with you forever; through Jesus Christ, our Lord, who lives and reigns with you and the Holy Spirit, one God, now and forever. **Amen.**

Pentecost 26

Year A

Lord God, humble us by your Holy Spirit to keep in mind the end of all things and the Day of Judgment. Stir us to holiness of life and, at the Last Day, exalt us to live with you forever; through your Son, Jesus Christ our Lord, who lives and reigns with you in the unity of the Holy Spirit, one God, now and forever. **Amen.**

Year B

Lord Jesus, our Judge and King, your first coming as our Savior encourages us to endure through the tumult of fearsome days, and your death assures us that we are secure in God's love. Give us grace to endure faithfully, confident that, even in the midst of chaos, you will use our lives to continue your ministry in the world. You live and reign with the Father and the Holy Spirit, one God, now and forever. **Amen.**

Year C

O God, alert us to the signs of the end of all things, prepare us for the coming of the Son of Man, absolve us from our offenses, free us from the bonds of our sins, and deliver us by your bountiful goodness; through Jesus Christ, your Son, our Lord, who lives and reigns with you and the Holy Spirit, one God, now and forever. **Amen.**

Pentecost 27

Year A

Purify our consciences, Almighty God, by your daily visitation that, when your Son returns, he will find in us faith that is active in love, prepared to receive him who lives and reigns with you and the Holy Spirit, one God, now and forever. **Amen.**

Year B

Lord Jesus, our Judge and King, you will come again with great power and glory to gather your people to your side. Give us grace to trust your Word, which will not pass away. Help us to live purposefully in our world, knowing you not only as Judge and King, but also as Savior and Lord. You live and reign with the Father and the Holy Spirit, one God, now and forever. **Amen.**

Year C

Almighty and ever-living God, since you have given exceedingly great and precious promises to those who believe, grant us so perfectly and without all doubt to believe in your Son Jesus Christ that our faith in your sight may never be reproved; through the same Jesus Christ, who lives and reigns with you and the Holy Spirit, one God, now and forever. **Amen.**

Third-Last Sunday in the Church Year

Year A

O God, your Son came into the world to destroy the works of the devil and to make us your children and heirs of eternal life. When he comes again with power, make us like him, for we shall see him as he is, who lives and reigns with you and the Holy Spirit, one God, now and forever. **Amen.**

Year B

Lord Jesus, our Judge and King, your first coming as our Savior encourages us to endure through the tumult of fearsome days and assures us that we are secure in your love. Help us to endure faithfully and give us confidence that, even in the midst of chaos, you will use our lives to continue your ministry in the world. You live and reign with the Father and the Holy Spirit, one God, now and forever. **Amen.**

Year C

O God, your kingdom is present among us in the Gospel and in the Sacraments. Prepare us for the coming of the Son of Man, absolve us from our offenses, free us from the bonds of our sins, and deliver us by your bountiful goodness; through Jesus Christ, your Son, our Lord, who lives and reigns with you and the Holy Spirit, one God, now and forever. **Amen.**

Second-Last Sunday in the Church Year

Year A

Merciful Creator, your hand is open wide to satisfy the needs of every living creature. Because we must one day give an account of ourselves, help us to use your good gifts faithfully; through Jesus Christ our Lord, who with you and the Holy Spirit, lives and reigns, one God, now and forever. **Amen.**

Year B

Lord Jesus, our Judge and King, you will come again with great power and glory to gather your people to your side. Give us grace to trust your Word, which will not pass away. Show us how to live purposefully in our world, serving you, our Savior and Lord, who lives and reigns with the Father and the Holy Spirit, one God, now and forever. **Amen.**

Year C

Almighty and ever-living God, since you have given exceedingly great and precious promises to those who believe, grant us so perfectly and without all doubt to believe in your Son Jesus Christ that our faith in your sight may never be reproved; through our Savior, Jesus Christ, who lives and reigns with you and the Holy Spirit, one God, now and forever. **Amen.**

SUNDAY OF THE FULFILLMENT
Last Sunday in the Church Year

Year A

Almighty and merciful God, it is your gift that we offer you true and faithful worship. Prepare us to recognize your Son when he comes again, receiving from his hand the joy of eternal life. He lives and reigns with you and the Holy Spirit, one God, now and forever. **Amen.**

Year B

Lord Jesus Christ, King of the universe, one day you will come in power and great glory, and we will see Eden's bliss restored. O Wisdom, ruling all things mightily and tenderly, gather together all your people to live with you forever; for you live and reign with the Father and the Holy Spirit, one God, now and forever. **Amen.**

Year C

Lord God, Heavenly Father, you have made us stewards of the riches of your grace. Prepare us to meet our Lord when he comes again in glory and preserve our faith as we hold fast to the blessed hope of everlasting life; through Jesus Christ, your Son, our Lord, who lives and reigns with you and the Holy Spirit, one God, now and forever. **Amen.**

Christ the King

Year A

Almighty and everlasting God, it is your will to restore all things to your beloved Son, whom you anointed King of all creation. Unite all the people of the earth, now divided by the power of sin, under the glorious and gentle rule of our Lord Jesus Christ, who lives and reigns with you and the Holy Spirit, one God, now and forever. **Amen.**

Year B

Lord Jesus Christ, King of the universe, when you come in power and glory, we will see Eden's bliss restored. O Wisdom, rule all things mightily and tenderly and gather together all your people to live with you forever; for you live and reign with the Father and the Holy Spirit, one God, now and forever.

Year C

Lord God, Heavenly Father, send forth your Son, the Christ of God to lead home his bride, the Church, to the paradise he has graciously prepared; and receive us, and all the redeemed, into your eternal kingdom; through Jesus Christ, your Son, our Lord, who lives and reigns with you and the Holy Spirit, one God, now and forever. **Amen.**

Festivals and Days of Special Devotion

Christmas Eve

O Almighty God, you have made this night to shine with the brightness of the true Light, Jesus Christ, your only Son. Give us great joy in the angels' message of peace on earth and lead each of us to receive Jesus as God-with-us, our Emmanuel. This we ask for his love's sake. **Amen.**

Christmas Day

Gracious God, we celebrate this day of our Lord's birth as the fulfillment of your promise of redemption from sin. We welcome you, Jesus, as the Savior of the world and the Lord of our hearts, who now lives and rules with the Father and the Holy Spirit, one God, world without end. **Amen.**

Second Sunday after Christmas

Almighty Father, you have shined on us the new light of your Word made flesh, who lived among us. Cause Jesus, this Light, kindled in our hearts, to shine through our lives; through the same Jesus Christ, our Lord, who lives and reigns with you and the Holy Spirit, one God, now and forever. **Amen.**

Epiphany

O God, by a star you led the Wise Men of old to worship the Christ child. So lead us that we too may worship him in all our lives. Holy Spirit within us, guide our works and shape our deeds and actions into fit expressions of worship, praise, and love. This we ask in the name of Jesus, the Light of the world. **Amen.**

Ash Wednesday

Gracious and merciful God, you forgive the sins of all who come to you with penitent and contrite hearts. Grant us the spirit of true repentance to acknowledge our sins and to find in you forgiveness and restoration, wholeness, and peace; through the merits of Jesus Christ our Lord and our Redeemer. **Amen.**

Good Friday

Blessed are you, O Lord our God, King of the universe. You have poured out upon us your never-ending love by giving your Son, Jesus Christ, into death on the cross for us. Give us grace to know nothing except Jesus Christ and him crucified. Strengthen the ministry of your Church to bring Jesus' love to all those for whom he died. For he lives and reigns with you and the Holy Spirit, one God, now and forever. **Amen.**

Holy Saturday/Easter Eve

Blessed Lord Jesus Christ, as Nicodemus and Joseph showed care for your body after it had hung on the cross, we also want to show care for your body, the Church. By the indwelling of your Spirit, strengthen us in our baptismal vows and make us the sign of your presence in this world, testifying to the power of the resurrection and the joy of the life to come. In your precious name we pray. **Amen.**

Ascension

O King of glory, on this day you ascended in triumph far above all heavens. We ask your Spirit's abiding presence here on earth, within our hearts. Empower us truly to be your disciples in this life and to be your companions at the heavenly feast for all eternity. This we ask for your love's sake. **Amen.**

Reformation

O Holy Spirit, you direct the Church in every age. Guide us in our generation to be bold in our witness to the Gospel and faithful and clear in our confession of the faith entrusted to us, freely and joyfully sharing the Good News of our Lord, Jesus Christ, whom with you and the Father we worship, one God, now and forever. **Amen.**

Saints

Apostles

Almighty God, Caller and Sender of people of faith in every age, we bless you for the Apostles, who in their time faithfully spread the Gospel of salvation. By your Holy Spirit continue their work through us, so that at last we too may hear you say, "Well done, faithful servant." This we ask in the name of Jesus Christ, your Son, our Lord. **Amen.**

Evangelists

Lead us, eternal God, to treasure the testimony to our blessed Lord Jesus Christ written by the Evangelists. Help us to find in the Gospels eternal truth and the way of salvation. Speak your living words to our hearts from each chapter and verse. This we ask in the name of your Son and our Savior. **Amen.**

Men and Women of Faith

Inspire us, God of the ages, by the lives of men and women of faith from ages past, especially your servant[s] _____. Help us to learn from their witness, to honor their contributions to our heritage, and to consider their examples as we follow Jesus Christ, our leader and our master, in this our generation. In His abiding name we pray. **Amen.**

Life of the Church

Congregational Anniversary

Gracious God, we bless you for this milestone in the life of our congregation, [*briefly identify it*]. We thank you for the dedication and devotion of members and friends, past and present, who labored in your name. By the Holy Spirit's presence and power we commit ourselves to continue working together to your glory; in the name of Jesus Christ, your Son. **Amen.**

Dedication

Lord of life and Giver of all good gifts, with thanksgiving and joy we dedicate this _____ to your praise and glory. Show us new ways to respond to your unending love, that the sharing of our lives and our goods will be a continuing reflection of the blessings you so richly grant us. This we ask in the name of Jesus Christ, your greatest gift. **Amen.**

Celebration

God of time and space, of love and laughter, you have made us for your pleasure. We are gathered in Jesus' name to celebrate _____. Bless us with your Spirit's presence, and make this party an earthly preview of the wedding feast in heaven that your Son, Jesus Christ, our Lord, is preparing for us. **Amen.**

Life of the Christian

Birth/Adoption of a Child

Gracious and merciful God, in your loving care you place us in families. We thank you for the nurture you provide for us throughout our earthly lives. Today we bless you for adding a child/children, [*names*(s)], to the circle of the [*name*] family. May this child/these children find joyful acceptance and a lasting welcome there. By the working of your Spirit draw all of us ever closer together in true unity in faith, in hope, and in charity. This we pray in the name of Jesus, our brother and our Lord. **Amen.**

Marriage

Almighty God, Creator and Shaper of our lives, we bless you for the joys of marriage, through which a man and a woman, sharing together in your love, find meaning and fulfillment. We thank you for the commitment to married love and mutual respect [*names*] have made. May their lives together as husband and wife know your full and rich benediction, as we also support them with our love, our concern, and our prayers. This we ask in the name of Jesus Christ. **Amen.**

Wedding Anniversary

Lord of all our seasons and our years, we thank you for the blessings of married life. Today we rejoice with [*names*] as they observe their [*number*] wedding anniversary. Continue to bless them, Heavenly Father, so that faithfulness to you and devotion to each other will be the hallmarks of all their life together. By your presence gladden each day that you graciously grant them. In the name of Jesus we pray. **Amen.**

Holidays

New Year

Gracious God of endings and beginnings, we commit to your grace and forgiveness the year now completed and commend to your kindness and love the year now beginning. Throughout the coming weeks and months make the presence of your Holy Spirit known in our lives, drawing us ever closer to Jesus, our Lord and our Redeemer, in whose wondrous name we make all of our beginnings. **Amen.**

National Holiday

Lord of time and God of history, we ask you to keep our nation and its leaders under your care. It is by your grace and blessing alone that we can know peace and freedom. Direct and lead us to live justly with our neighbors, peaceably in our communities and joyfully in our land, seeking the common good. This we ask through Jesus Christ, your Son, our Lord. **Amen.**

Thanksgiving

Lord of seedtime and of harvest, we thank you for the blessings you grant to the earth in each season. We rejoice in the wonderful richness of the land and in the astounding variety of food it produces to delight and satisfy us. We ask for one thing more, the willingness to share our blessings, so that all the earth can rejoice in your generosity. This we ask in the great name of Jesus. **Amen.**